# JUNIOR PET CARE

## KOI
## FOR PONDS

**ZUZA VRBOVA**

**Photography** Hugh Nicholas
**Illustration** Robert McAulay
**Reading and Child Psychology Consultant**
Dr. David Lewis

# ACKNOWLEDGMENTS

With special thanks to Neil Porter and Andrew Lindsey, Langley's Aquatics, and Mr. S. Lay.

**Library of Congress #89-52058**

Distributed in the UNITED STATES by T.F.H. Publications, Inc., One T.F.H. Plaza, Neptune City, NJ 07753; in CANADA to the Pet Trade by H & L Pet Supplies Inc., 27 Kingston Crescent, Kitchener, Ontario N2B 2T6; Rolf C. Hagen Ltd., 3225 Sartelon Street, Montreal 382 Quebec; in CANADA to the Book Trade by Macmillan of Canada (A Division of Canada Publishing Corporation), 164 Commander Boulevard, Agincourt, Ontario M1S 3C7; in ENGLAND by T.F.H. Publications, The Spinney, Parklands, Portsmouth PO7 6AR; in AUSTRALIA AND THE SOUTH PACIFIC by T.F.H. (Australia) Pty. Ltd., Box 149, Brookvale 2100 N.S.W., Australia; in NEW ZEALAND by Ross Haines & Son, Ltd., 82 D Elizabeth Knox Place, Panmure, Auckland, New Zealand; in the PHILIPPINES by Bio-Research, 5 Lippay Street, San Lorenzo Village, Makati, Rizal; in SOUTH AFRICA by Multipet Pty. Ltd., P.O. Box 35347, Northway, 4065, South Africa. Published by T.F.H. Publications, Inc. Manufactured in the United States of America by T.F.H. Publications, Inc.

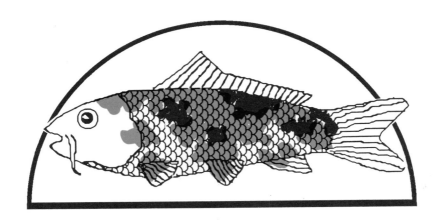

# CONTENTS

## NOTE TO PARENTS

Youngsters will never stop appreciating the beauty of koi.
Children love to watch their koi glistening and darting
across the garden pond, bringing constant life to the
water. This book has been designed to help young
children understand koi so that a parent and child can
share the wonderfully relaxing and ever-absorbing
experience of koi-keeping.

It has been specially written for children of age 7 years
and upwards and gently introduces children to the art of
koi-keeping. KOI FOR PONDS provides an initial
glimpse of the pleasure of what may become a lifelong
hobby.

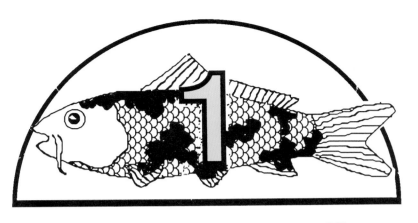

# THE PLEASURE
# OF KOI

The word koi comes from the Japanese word *Nishiki Goi*. *Nishiki* is Japanese for a very
colorful cloth
and

*Goi* means carp, which
is an ordinary fish. Koi are simply a
colorful kind of carp. Carp are fresh-
water fish. They do not live in the sea
but are found in lakes and rivers in
many places.

In Japan people used to eat ordinary brown carp. It is a good food
and is eaten in many countries.
Sometimes, long ago, some of the
brown carp were born with red or
blue patches on them. The Japanese
noticed this and they used these colored carp fish to raise even more colorful fish. By picking out the most at-
tractive fish and mating them, the
best features of each fish were high-
lighted. Soon the Japanese succeeded

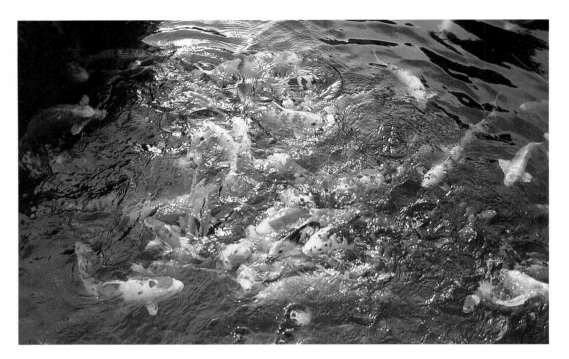

**Koi are like swimming jewels (above).**

in making a carp look like an especially beautiful fish—called koi.

If you look after your koi well and feed them properly, they will grow very large. Over a period of about five years, your koi could grow from being the size of your hand to being as long as your arm.

In Japan, koi have become greatly respected fish. They are symbols of happiness and they are thought to bring good luck. The oldest koi in Japan is red in color and called Hanako. She is believed to be 226 years old. To prove her great age, her scales were examined under a microscope. This great age is unusual although koi do live for a long time. In general, if they are looked after well, they live until they are about 70.

Koi come in a very exciting range of colors. They can be one bright color, for example gold, or several colors—red, blue and black can be seen on the body of one fish. The scales on the body of the fish can have different patterns too.

Keeping koi in your garden pond

**The colors of koi are stunning and you will never stop appreciating their beauty.**

**There are lots of different kinds and styles of ponds. You do not need a huge pond to keep your koi in. It can be very small, as long as the water is deep enough for the size of your koi.**

will make your garden an enchanting place to be in. The beauty of koi, dashing across the calm of the water will make your pond an even more eye-catching feature than it already is.

Each koi is like a unique, moving painting. Watching the array of color glistening in the sunlight will always be a compelling sight for you, your family and friends. Besides providing an unending picture show, koi are lots of fun to keep in other ways too. You will never become bored with feeding them. If you look after them well, they can become so tame and used to you that they even come to the surface of the water to let you stroke them.

# KOI AS A FISH

To be able to care for your koi properly you need to know a little about how fish live in water. Just like you and I, fish need to breathe and eat. They stay healthy by swimming in clean, fresh water.

Koi are chubby fish, with a high back. Their mouth points forward and they have fleshy lips.

When you first look at a koi you will quickly notice that, unlike gold-fish, they have what looks like a moustache at the sides of their mouths. This is really two pairs of barbels—fleshy "whiskers" pieces on their upper lip.

Koi do not have teeth in their mouth, but they do have teeth farther back towards their throat. Their teeth are used as a sieve to sift tiny animals from the water for the koi to eat.

Some koi are not patterned but come in one single color. This shiny, elegant-looking fish (above) is called a Kujaku.

**The muscular tail** drives the fish forward and helps it to change direction in the water. Koi have a single fin across their backs called the **dorsal fin** which helps to stop the fish from rolling over. The rest of the fins on a koi's body help to steer.

## THE FEATURES OF A KOI

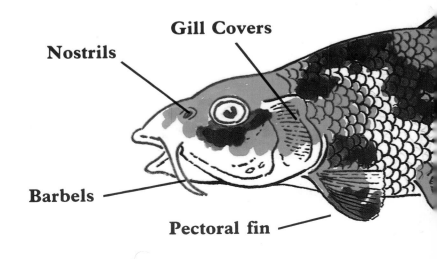

Gill Covers

Nostrils

Barbels

Pectoral fin

**The gills** are used for breathing. They are rather like our lungs. Gills are very delicate and are covered by a gill cover which you can easily see. It is near the head of the fish. As the gills can be damaged or infected, it is important for you to keep a close check on this part of the koi's body.

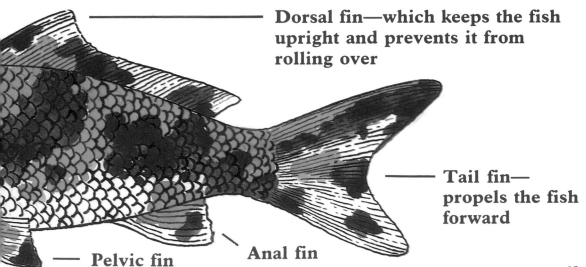

Dorsal fin—which keeps the fish upright and prevents it from rolling over

Tail fin— propels the fish forward

Pelvic fin

Anal fin

# A KOI'S SENSES

Koi have keen eyesight, but their eyes do not have lids. A koi uses its nostrils to smell and find food. Their sense of smell is backed up by taste buds in the barbels around the mouth. As the koi looks for food, it uses its barbels like antennae to distinguish between food and rubbish that might be found at the bottom of a pond.

Koi can hear well. They do not have good ears, but their body senses sound waves in the water.

**The body** of a koi is covered in three kinds of outer layer. There is epidermis skin on the outside, then scales and then the endodermis or the skin attached to the flesh. These layers protect the fish and if they are damaged, it could easily become ill.

**Koi's scales** are sometimes unlike the scales of the common wild carp. The scales can vary in size and shape.

The Japanses have raised some koi to have large scales, some with small scales and some with no scales at all. A koi with only a few large glossy scales is called **Doitsu.** This is the Japanese word meaning German. Doitsu koi are influenced by a carp that first appeared in Germany with this unusual scale pattern. It was eventually sent to Japan.

**The scales of a koi help to protect the fish as well as making it look pretty.**

# THE DIFFERENT
# KINDS OF
# KOI

All koi are one
kind of fish but they
vary in the color and the pattern of
their skin. Until recently, most of the
koi we have were brought to the
United States and Europe from Japan. Nowadays, some koi are born
and raised locally.

You will soon become familiar with
the kinds of colors and color combinations that koi come in. The Japanese have given each color and pattern
combination a name.

The names are built up from simple terms that denote color, pattern
and similarity to natural things—such
as plants. Some of the names refer to
periods of Japanese history that the
koi were developed in. For example
there is a popular kind of fish called
**Taisho Sanke.** Taisho is the name of
a Japanese emperor, and this koi was
produced during his rule. Sanke

**A Kin Matsuba** means the fish has three different colors. A Taisho Sanke fish has a white body with a red and black pattern on it.

Koi can also be named after an animal. A **Tancho** is named after a Japanese white-bodied bird which has a red head.

Being able to recognize the different kinds of koi and learning their names is an exciting part of koi-keeping. The names are easy to pronounce and you will soon

find that the Japanese words are rolling off your tongue. Knowing the names of the fish opens up a whole new world of words.

Being able to identify a fish by its appearance is like knowing the name of a plant. You will be able to discuss the beauty of your koi with your friends and family. You can compare the colors and special features of your fish with others that your friends might have. This will make koi-keeping even more fun.

**A Shiro Utsuri is a fish with two colors— snow white markings on a black skin. A Ki Utsuri would look similar to this but have a yellow pattern on black skin.**

# POPULAR VARIETIES OF KOI

The koi featured on this page is a fish
of one color—a Platinum Oghon. It has
a beautiful body but the small yellow
area around the eye is not a desirable
feature.

This koi with three different colors—white, red and
blue, is called an Ai-Goromo. The Hi (red) scales
have blue borders which make an interesting netlike

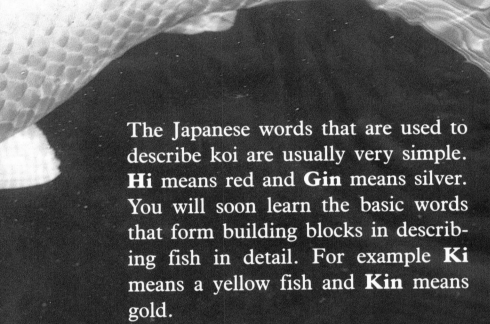

The Japanese words that are used to describe koi are usually very simple. **Hi** means red and **Gin** means silver. You will soon learn the basic words that form building blocks in describing fish in detail. For example **Ki** means a yellow fish and **Kin** means gold.

Once you are familiar with the names, you and your friends will be able to compare fish easily and can look forward to collecting and choosing new fish with different color combinations.

**A Platinum Oghon can sometimes be called Parachina Oghon.**

A **Kohaku** is a popular koi with a white body, overlaid with a red pattern. If it has a red mouth and looks as if it is wearing lipstick, it is called a Kuchibeni Kohaku.

A **Showa Sanke** has a black body with a red and white pattern. Showa refers to the Emperor Showa era in Japan, during which this fish was produced.

A **Tancho Kohaku** is a simple and elegant-looking fish (below). It is a white koi with a round Hi (red) marking on the head. As its colors are only white and red, it reminds Japanese people of their national flag. The round Hi markings should not spread over the eyes or shoulders but should be as large and as round as possible. The black and white tail (right) is part of a **Shiro Utsuri.**

## A SHOWA SANKE AND A TAISHO SANKE

**The easiest way** to understand the difference between a **Showa Sanke** and a **Taisho Sanke** is to imagine you were painting the body of the koi yourself. For a Taisho Sanke fish, you would have a white background and paint the red and black patterns on top of the white. With a Showa Sanke you would start off with black paper and paint white and red designs on it.

The **Doitsu Sanke** shown on this page has Hi (red) and Sumi (black) markings on a white skin and has two lines of big scales. It is like a Taisho Sanke fish in that it has three colors—red and black on a snow white background.

The black and red markings on the body, ideally, should be well balanced and any black scales or specks on the snow white skin are not desirable.

A Doitsu Hariwake. It has two rows of large scales. You can see one row down the side and one row along the top of its body. This kind of koi has orange markings on a metallic, silvery colored background.

**An Ai-Goromo (top) swimming over a Shiro-Utsuri.**

In general, koi are regarded as being very expensive. But baby koi are cheap, and if you choose a good small youngster (left), it may well grow up to be a prize-winning and valuable koi (right).

## A HEALTHY KOI

The body should be glistening with no damaged patches on its surface. Overall, your chosen koi should look well fed and well kept.

The fish that you choose should be swimming about actively and effortlessly. All its fins should be well spread. The eyes should be bright and clear.

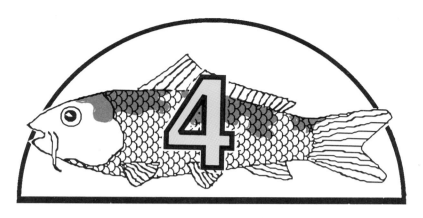

# BUYING A KOI

**When koi are young, koi dealers put them in special ponds. The koi are priced according to their size and color.**

It is hard to predict what a young koi will look like in a few years' time. Even a person who is experienced in buying koi will not be able to tell what a fish will look like in the future.

This is because koi colors take up to five years to fully develop. During this time, some colors may fade, while others darken.

Whichever koi you choose, it is most sensible to choose one that looks healthy and lively. Its colors should show the color pattern you are looking for. It may stay the same color and if you feed it well, the colors may become even brighter.

Fish need the oxygen in the air to breathe—just as we do. To make sure that your fish does not suffocate in the plastic bag on the way home, many koi dealers fill in the bag with oxygen from an oxygen tank.

**Your koi is now ready to be taken home—in the bag containing some water, air and additional oxygen. If you prefer, you can bring a plastic bucket with a tight-fitting lid to carry your koi home in.**

# CHOOSING YOUR KOI

Selecting a young, healthy-looking koi.

Most koi dealers will put your new koi into a plastic bag for you to carry it home in.

The bag with the koi in it is not filled full with water because oxygen will be added.

Do not put a new koi straight into your pond. Float the bag on the surface for about half an hour first.

# HOW TO HANDLE YOUR KOI

If you have to pick a koi up, it is important for you to wet your hands first. Using dry hands could damage the slimy covering on the fish and make it ill. Hold the fish gently, cradling the body with both hands.

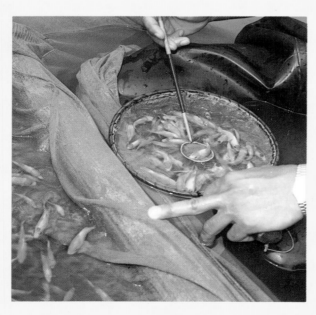

Using a net to take a koi out of the water can damage the koi's fins and may remove some scales. It is best just to guide the fish with the net in the water and then gently transfer the fish into a plastic bowl or tub.

## Arriving home

If you already have other koi you should have a specially prepared, temporary container for your new fish. If you do not have any other fish you can put your new koi straight into its permanent home.

Float the bucket or bag with the fish in it on the surface of your pond for a while.

You should do this so that the temperature of the two kinds of water can adjust to each other. This way, your fish will not get a shock and is not upset when it is placed in its new home.

## When to buy koi

Spring is the best time of year to buy koi. The warmer months which lie ahead will encourage the fish to eat and grow. Fish that have traveled from Japan will be hungry when they arrive. In winter, they will find it harder to become strong again and get used to the new conditions.

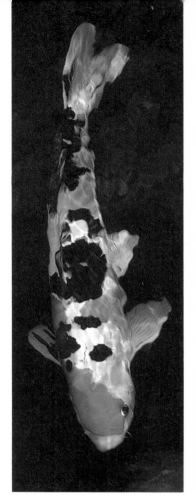

**A Doitsu Sanke**

# FEEDING
# YOUR KOI

Koi are easily tamed and when they eat out of your hand they can become very lovable. Fish, like most creatures, like to have a variety of food. You can buy the ideal food for your koi in most pet stores. It usually comes in pellets that are easy to feed. Pellets contain all the foods needed to keep koi healthy.

**You can buy everything you need to care for your koi from aquarium stores.**

### Koi pellets

You can buy different kinds of pellets to suit the size of your fish and the season. Small, young koi will find large pellets difficult to eat, so you should buy small-sized pellets for youngsters.

# DIFFERENT KINDS OF KOI PELLETS

Small 'mini' wheat germ pellets for winter feeding (left)

Some pellets contain the correct balanced diet for koi during the summer.

**As a tasty treat** and as a change from fish pellets, you can sometimes feed your koi worms that you find in the garden. Your koi will lift its head out of the water and take the worm from your hand.

Koi do not have stomachs like ours, so they cannot eat much at a time. It is better to feed small, fre-

**Basic, large staple pellets for feeding large fish during summer (right) and special winter feed pellets (below).**

quent meals. Any food that the koi do not eat should be removed because otherwise the remains will slowly go bad and poison the water. Any left-over food will make the water dirty. This will make it more difficult to see your koi and appreciate them. Any food that you give your koi should be eaten up completely, while you are feeding them. Ideally, it should be eaten within three minutes.

**A koi's appetite** depends on the temperature of the water. When the water is warm, the koi will eat more food. During very cold weather, koi

**'Mini-gold' pellets (right) can be mixed with normal pellets in summer to improve your koi's colors.**

become inactive and do not eat. They lie at the bottom of the pond in a semi-dormant state. This means that they are half-asleep, using very little energy and needing very little food, if any.

## Bringing out the colors

Sometimes, the colors of a koi can fade but you can help to keep their colors bright by feeding your koi with specially-prepared foods that will make their colors stronger.

Some koi pellets have been developed that not only help the koi to grow and to stay healthy but help to make their colors sparkle. These foods contain ingredients such as car-

**Koi jump so high out of the water when they are fed that you must protect them from any cats that might try to catch your koi.**

Some koi have nicknames and come to their keeper when they are called.

otene. This is what gives carrots their bright orange color and in the same way will brighten a koi's natural colors.

Another kind of pellet contains spirulina. This is a tiny plant that flamingos eat that keeps their feathers bright pink. A spirulina-based pellet can be mixed with regular food and fed to improve the red color. Color-enhancing pellets should only be used as a supplement to your koi's usual feed.

## Going on vacation

Although koi do appreciate your company they are independent creatures. They can be left safely without food for a week or two. A complete break from being fed is sometimes good for koi.

As your fish grow you will find koi ever more fascinating and challenging to keep. This is not only because koi are so surprisingly gentle and tame but because you have so much control over your koi's coloring and growth. The original color, size and shape of the fish is defined when you buy it, but koi are like plants—you can strengthen their features and size by the kind of food and care you give. Remember, every koi is like a moving painting and as each one is different, each keeper can be proud of his or her own individual koi.

**It is best to decide on a certain place for feeding your koi. They gather when they hear your footsteps.**

# GLOSSARY

**Barbels** Short, whisker-like extensions which grow from the lip of the fish and are used like antennae to search for food.

**Carotene** Vitamin substance used in certain koi pellets to enhance the fish's colors.

**Doitsu** A native German pond goldfish with a few large glossy scales.

**Dorsal fin** The single fin on the back. (Some fishes have more than one dorsal fin.)

**Gill** Used for breathing, the gills are the equivalent of human lungs.

**Gin** The Japanese word for the color silver.

**Hi** The Japanese word for the color red.

**Ki** The Japanese word for the color yellow.

**Kin** The Japanese word for the color gold.

**Kin Ki Utsuri** A gold, yellow and black pond goldfish.

**Kohaku** A white-bodied pond goldfish with red overlays.

**Koi** Japanese pond goldfish, a member of the carp family distinguished by its bright colors.

**Showa Sanke** A black-bodied fish with red and white patterns.

**Spirulina** A tiny plant used in certain koi pellets to enhance colors.

**Sumi** The Japanese word for the color black.

**Taisho Sanke** A pond goldfish named for the Japanese emperor Taisho, and the fact that it has three colors, Sanke.

**Tancho** A pond goldfish named after a Japanese bird which is white with a red head, much like the fish's coloration.